THE WAY OF

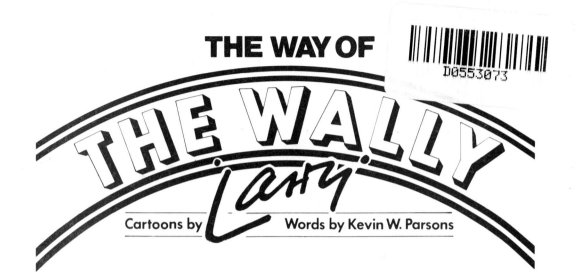

THE WALLY

Larry

Cartoons by **Larry**   Words by Kevin W. Parsons

CENTURY PUBLISHING
LONDON

Foreword

Hello,
You know all of us at some time or another think we're a bit of a Wally. I know I do. And I know my friends do too. In fact I'm certain they do because every time I see them they always say 'You're a bit of a Wally aren't you!', and offer to buy me a pint of Double Diamond.

But now the time has come for Wallies everywhere to stand up and be counted. Or rather don't stand up, stay sitting down where you are in front of the television with the sound turned on full and a packet of Jacobs Cheddars by your side. We'll send someone along to count you in the comfort of your own home, providing that is you've actually got a comfortable home, with a front door that has one of those nice wrought-iron panels behind the glass, and a hall light in the form of a chandelier, and a quilted bed head that's gone all funny where the heads have touched it, and a four-year-old Honda Civic parked in the car port outside.

Because, and I speak to you all here, because it's time we Wallies weren't afraid to say 'I'm A Wally and proud of it!' After all, what's wrong with wearing clothes bought in the Marks & Spencer sale?

So Wallies everywhere, especially in Coventry, Basingstoke and Wales, the time has come to raise your anorak hoods high and go about your business.

Thank you. And may your Hush Puppies go with you!

Dictated into a dictating machine when it was switched off by

THE PRESIDENT
The World Convention of Wallies

The History of The Wally

Opinion varies as to when the first Wally came to Britain. Many regard the Celts as the first true Wallies. Certainly the Wally links with Celtic Supporters Club are still strong today. Others regard the Normans as the first real Wallies and point to the fact that Norman is a very, very Wally sort of a name.

Whatever their origin, it seems certain that the Wallies had arrived in Britain by the mid-seventeenth century. It may be safely assumed that from then on most of the population were complete Wallies. The eighteenth century saw an even greater expansion of the Wally Movement (which is generally very fast and wobbly). The Industrial Revolution was now at hand and Wally inventors were vital to its success. Men such as Wally Stephenson, Wally Hargreaves and Wally Arkwright have become legends in their own right.

When Victoria took to the throne, the country could look forward to more expansion in Wally behaviour culminating in that most Wally of institutions – the British Empire.

The 1950s, however, saw perhaps the greatest achievements: the portable plastic garage, the non-stick budgie tray and the flip-flop sandal. Now into the eighties, the spirit of the true Wally is still with us, especially in New Zealand, Scandinavia, Scandinavia and Scandinavia, and we can look forward to a rich and Wally future!

Early Days . . . a poem

I was born a Wally
A Wally is what I am
If I hadn't been born a Wally
I'd probably have been a civil engineer.
                                        A. Wally

The Formative Years

The formative years for most Wallies are between 15½ and 16, coincidental with that all-important first discovery of the zip-up cardigan, and at a time when other people of the same age are discovering members of the opposite sex. It is at this age that Wallies consume their first alcohol, traditionally in the form of Campari and lemonade, a drink which produces instant nausea and a bad headache. This is the age, too, when Wallies first start going to parties (generally without an invitation), where they usually end up in the kitchen talking to the cuckoo clock.

The formative years also see the first move into paid employment with a Saturday job behind the bacon counter at Dewhurst's. Watch out for the first growth of facial hair, sometimes on the chin or upper lip, but quite often on the tip of the nose. Watch out, too, for long spells in the bathroom during which the Wally discovers that all important 'great smell of Brut' for the first time. Other points to note include a desire to stay up later than 7pm during the week and the dawning realisation that happiness might well come from something other than owning a new BMX bike.

Motor Cars . . . a poem

I wish I was a motor car
Cortina sixteen hundred E
I'd give myself a cosmic paint job,
Four stick-on wheel trims, well maybe three,
Inside I'd hang a lucky horseshoe,
A woolly dice, a gonk, a bee,
Then four miles on I'd hit a lamp post
And all because I couldn't see.

                                        Arnold

The Wally on Three Wheels

No aspect of modern life offers quite so many opportunities to the Wally as does the open road, whether it be a steady 30 mph down the middle lane of the M4 in a 'K' registration Simca, or an unsteady 90 mph through some sleepy Suffolk village in a brand new BMW turbo. Motoring Wallies fall into three categories:

The Cruiser Class Wally   His one aim is to travel everywhere at a steady 30 mph, never mind the consequences and never mind the fact that he's never been able to park the car in any space smaller than the average-size bus garage.

The Destroyer Class Wally   His one aim is to arrive anywhere two minutes before he set off. His only contact with other motorists is a bumper bar thrust angrily up the right-hand brake light of the car in front.

Other Wallies . . .   include anyone who stops to use a road atlas while positioned at a busy 'T' junction, anyone who requires a clear three-lane passage to get past a parked obstacle, and anyone who last used the footbrake in 1947.

Cars

'I happen to think that the Datsun Cherry happens
to be one of the most stylish and elegant cars
on the road today.'

Auto Wally

Wally Cars to Be Seen In

* Reliant Robin
* Ford Anglia with wide wheels and tinted windows
* Skodas
* Ladas
* Ford Corsair (especially with dangling dice and purple furry dashboard)
* Any BL car, but especially
  Mustard-coloured Allegros
  Princess/Ambassador
  Maxi (expecially with roof rack and blowing exhaust)
  Triumph Acclaim
* Vauxhall Viva SL

* Fiat Panda
* Anything that has a 'My Other Car's A Porsche' sticker in the rear window
* Anything that gets overtaken by a man pushing a bicycle
* Anything that involves the name Talbot
* Polski Fiat
* Renault 4
* Converted GPO vans
* Unconverted GPO vans
* Anything with a trailer
* Hillman Imp

Wally Things to Fasten to Your Car

* Anything at all that dangles

* Anything electrical that clips onto the dashboard and drains all the power away from the engine, cutting performance by half

* A gadget for calculating exact fuel consumption

* Anything at all that fastens onto a tow bar

* Anything that fastens onto the roof and later falls off the roof and into the path of anything at all that fastens onto the tow bar

* Any sticker that makes reference to sexual, athletic or financial prowess

* A carpet for the boot

* An attachment that fits into the car cigar lighter socket and enables you to run a small electric manicure set for up to twelve hours non-stop

* Clip-on plastic picnic trays for driver and passenger

* Seat covers made out of artificial fur which slip over front and rear seats

* Go-faster stripes you can stick on the side of your car to make it look more sporty and which you then tear off because they don't look quite sporty enough, only to take off a strip of brand new paint all the way down the side of the car

* Any device that tells you when you are running out of Yorkie bars

✳ Health and Fitness

There can be few sights more typical of the Wally than the first lemon-green blur of an early morning tracksuit as it flashes by on a crisp winter morning. Look out for the brand name sweat bands on the arms, wrists, head, legs and ankles. Also look out for the Tesco 'own brand' training shoes. Wallies generally chain smoke when jogging; watch out for the King Size pack of Marlboro bulging in the tracksuit bottoms.

Wallies rarely pursue any course of exercise for long. Thus the jogger quickly turns to rugby, and then to soccer, tennis, swimming and golf, spending considerable amounts of money on kit which by tradition should be two sizes too large. Wallies rarely get beyond the club fifth team.

In team sports Wallies make enormous amounts of noise but seldom, if ever, come into contact with the ball – except when it hits them.

Exercises for Wallies

The exercise bicycle   Ideal for the Wally. Only a true Wally would consider spending hours pedalling away on a bicycle that doesn't go anywhere.

Roller skates   Ideal way to lose weight, teeth, etc. Best suited to Wallies who live on main roads and can gain extra fun trying to race French juggernauts.

Pogo Sticks   Especially well suited to wooden or polished floors where they may cause irreparable damage.

Skipping ropes   Few Wallies know how to use one properly, hence their popularity. Generally, they take four Wallies to operate – two to turn the rope, one to jump and one to call the ambulance.

Punchball   Few Wallies manage to go the full distance without being knocked out.

The Wally Exercise Schedule

✳

Monday   Wake up, get up, dress, shower, take off wet clothes, go back to bed.

Tuesday   Stand on spot, bring left knee up under left shoulder, bring right knee up under right shoulder, fall over, kick something, go down to the pub.

Wednesday Ten press ups, ten sit ups, ten knee bends, ten Rothmans.

Thursday Placing both feet firmly beneath the wardrobe or other heavy object, pull up smartly from the waist, bang head on freshly opened wardrobe door, recoil back in agony nursing cut forehead, sit on keys in back pocket, remove keys from back pocket, remove children from earshot, swear loudly.

Friday   Wake up, dress, clean someone else's teeth, put someone else's teeth into mouth, put someone else's handkerchief into mouth, remove teeth with someone else's handkerchief, give teeth to person they belong to, keep handkerchief.

Saturday Get up, go down to pub, come back from pub, go to bed.

Sunday   Run up and down on the spot for ten minutes, clutch leg in agony, shout 'cramp', fall over, cut leg on sideboard, break ankle, fracture pelvis, sever tendon, give up.

Work . . . a poem

What is work?
Work is
Something
I quite like doing
Except
When I put my hand inside
The machine
When
It is still going round
And then
I don't like it
Very much at all.

                                   Anon

Wally Places to Work

* Toyshops

* Any booking hall on British Rail Southern Region

* Unipart Service Counters

* Larger branches of Boots (especially on the Home Brewing Counter)

* The Post Office

* London Transport

* Any office of the Norwich Union Commercial Assurance Company

* Sealink

* British Telecom

* Anything at all to do with men's toiletries

* As a British Airways steward on the Super Shuttle

* As a Club 18–30 holiday courier

* As anything else to do with Club 18–30

* As a male nurse in a maternity home

* As a motorbike despatch rider

* As a community policoman

* Anywhere in Wales

* As a loft insulation salesman

* In a florist's

* As a traffic warden

* Designing the labels for knitting patterns

* In Sketchley's

* Teaching drama and movement to sixteen-year-olds

* As a manager at Wicks Superstores

* Modelling men's leisure and beachwear

* As a football commentator

Useful Wally Phrases for Work

*   A frank and useful dialogue

*   A mandate from the workers

*   We are united in our differences

*   The basis for compromise is on the table

*   The situation has become a situation in itself

*   Fundamental human principles are not negotiable

*   We have shown that we can work within given parameters when these given parameters are not unworkable

*   I consider this to be a victory for common sense

*   I do not agree that we are close to a settlement but that is not to say a settlement might not be just around the corner

Holidays . . . a poem

I like holidays
because
on holidays
I can do
lots of things
I can't do
at home
like . . .
getting caught out by the tide and having to call out the
lifeguard,
and smashing empty lemonade bottles on the beach and hiding
them just beneath the surface ready for someone to tread on,
and playing with a Frisbee near the kiddies' pool and frightening
all the children,
and bringing seaweed home to the caravan and keeping it
underneath the camp bed where it begins to smell like cold
sicky and spoils the holiday for everyone.

Darren

Wally Places to Go On Holiday

- ✳ * The Isle of Man
- * Brittany
- ✳ * Anywhere in North Wales
- * Anywhere with Club Pontinental
- ✳ * Anything that has 'Fun For All The Family' on the sign outside
- * Anywhere that can be reached by bus from home in under twenty minutes
- * Torbay
- * Anywhere that involves a 2 a.m. flight from Luton Airport
- * Anywhere on the East Coast of England
- ✳* Anywhere with Authentic Local Atmosphere
- ✳* Malham Cove during term time
- * Stevenage
- * Hanwell
- ✳ Anywhere that involves the use of a rucksack
- * Anywhere favoured by German tourists
- * Telford

Wally Things to Pack When Going On Holiday

* Home-made towelling robe

* Primus stove with individual cups and saucers

* Crochet-knit bikini which has stretched in the wash

* Sand

* Tube of sun-tan cream without a top on

* A large jar of Sandwich Spread without a top on

* Funny little plastic shield to stop the nose getting sunburnt which leaves a white line across both cheeks where the elastic has protected the skin from the sun

* Old football shorts

* Inflatable dinghy

* Plastic bathing ring made up in the style of an old car inner tube

* Loud transistor radio tuned in to Radio 1

* Snorkel and one flipper

* Rubber bathing cap bought in 1954

* Any T-shirt with your own name printed on the front

* Any T-shirt with someone else's name printed on the front

* Any beach ball that comes free with four gallons of petrol

* A copy of the *Tit-Bits* summer special

* A bath towel that doesn't quite cover you all over when you want to get changed

* A year's supply of Diocalm

* Twelve identical thick pullovers

* A briefcase

* A pair of shorts with the pockets showing below the edges

Some Holiday 'Do's and Don'ts'

Don't   bother when the lifeguard tells you it's unsafe to bathe because of the dangerous currents and insist he-has-another-think-coming-if-he-thinks-some-trumped-up-nancy-boy-in-a-pair-of-skimpy-swimming-trunks-is-going-to-stop-anyone-he-fancies-from-taking-a-dip-when-they-feel-like-it.

Do   arrive late at the beach to find all the parking spaces on the promenade gone. Spend the next three hours driving slowly up and down the front in the red-hot heat waiting until someone moves.

Don't   warn your children that the culvert they've just spent six hours blocking with sand to form a giant lake is in fact an effluent disposal pipe carrying raw untreated sewage from the nearby camping site.

Do   call the Air Sea Rescue services out to rescue a man whose hat has just blown off in the botanical gardens.

Don't   go for a trip round the harbour without eating three enormous crab sandwiches and a packet of cashew nuts first.

Wally Things to Do at a High Street Bank

*   Stand in the queue for twenty minutes doing nothing then start to fill in all the slips just as it's your turn

*   Ask the cashier to change a £1 note into a £1 coin

*   Play with the ball point pen fastened to a bit of string on the counter and snap it off

*   Drop half a chocolate eclair into the revolving tray where the money is supposed to go

*   Ask for the money in £1 notes, then just at the last moment change your mind and ask for it all in silver

*   Laugh when the security alarm goes off and the staff all dive for cover

*   Withdraw £5.47

*   Ask if you can see the manager, then when he comes out hide behind the counter and ask if he can see you

*   Try to use your cash card in the night-safe security box

*   Take a copy of every single free booklet available on the display racks

*   Try and steam up the glass partition between yourself and the cashier by breathing all over it

*   Work there

Wally Things to Do at Football Games

* Climb up the floodlight pylons

* Run into the crash barriers and, when they don't move, start trying to knock them down with your head

* Try to injure the opposing goalkeeper by throwing £5 notes at him

* Try to remove the opposing goalkeeper's head with a cunningly concealed 8-foot concrete girder

* Drink six pints of McEwans Export before the game

* Visit the bar at halftime to get a cup of hot Bovril. Lose your place in the crowd and then spill entire contents of cup over as many people as possible as you attempt to fight your way back

* Go on shouting 'Ug Ug Ug Ug Ug Ug!' in a loud voice whenever you see anyone you recognise and whenever your own team has possession of the ball

* Keep asking the man next to you what's happening

* Leave early to avoid the rush just before the vital last goal is scored

Wally Football Teams to Support

* Hereford United
* Notts County
* Shrewsbury
* Orient
* Bristol City
* Millwall
* Port Vale
* Lincoln City
* Mansfield Town
* Northampton Town
* Peterborough United
* England

Useful Phrases for Sportswallies

* 'The lads done magic'

* 'The lads didn't done magic'

* 'The lad what got the goal is better than Kevin Keegan was at his age'

* 'Terry passed to Terry who passed to Terry who slipped it past Terry, switched it to Terry who drove it past Terry and sent Terry the wrong way and scored . . . Terry'

* 'Archibald, Archibald, Archibald . . . Archibald, Archibald, Archibald'

* 'Our name is on the cup this year, Barry'

* 'Doesn't Bobby Charlton play for them anymore then?'

* 'A piece of clinical finishing by the fullback, Desmond'

Food . . . a poem

I felt a bit hungry
So I went into the kitchen
To see what there was there
But I didn't like the look of anything I could find there
So I went out
And had two kebabs with soya sauce
Three crispy pancake rolls
And a sweet and sour chicken with beanshoots
From that Chinkie
Where they say they once found a cat in the fridge
And after that I felt much better
Then I threw up.

Gary

Food for The Wally

* Chocolate and mint-flavoured ice cream
* Twiglets, especially when served from the bottom of a duffle bag
* Orange juice cartons that squirt drink all over you when you try to use them
* Nuttalls Mintoes
* Potted meat sandwiches
* Heinz tomato soup
* Gravy which can be eaten with a knife
* Any dish at all that involves chunky chicken pieces
* Anything that moves
* Kiwi-fruit-and-peanut-flavoured yoghurt
* Kraft Cheese Slices
* Curried Baked Beans in the family-size tin
* Any three-course meal that can be eaten with just a spoon
* HP Fruity Sauce
* Weetabix
* Birds Dream Topping
* Anything on anybody else's plate
* Anything at all that involves Instant Whip
* Meat balls
* Smash

Wally Drinks

* Tizer
* Watney's Red Barrel
* 2 litro bottles of lemonade that have to be consumed in one go
* Carling Black Label
* Woodpecker Cider
* Cup of tea with the tea bag still in it
* A pint of Double Diamond
* Coffeemate
* Undiluted Ribena
* Ovaltine
* Lemonade Shandy in a ring pull can
* Lemonade Shandy in a ring pull can, with the ring pulled off and dropped inside the can before you drink from it
* Californian red wine
* Liebfraumilch
* Glass of water that teeth were in last night
* Horlicks
* Any combination of the above

Wally Recipes

Beans On Toast (A Truly Classic Wally Dish)

* Place very large slice of bread under grill (get a friend to help you)
* Put unopened tin of beans into pan and heat for ten minutes
* Add water to pan just before it finally goes into meltdown
* Open tin
* Remove bread from under grill and empty beans onto bread
* Serve with a glass of Corona Cherryade

Toasted Cheese Sandwich

* To a slice of toasted bread add cream, pineapple chunks, salad dressing, more cheese, pork luncheon meat, salt, pepper and sugar (by mistake)
* Cook till topping melts and forms hard crusty deposit on the bottom of the grill pan
* Add half a jar of Branston pickle directly into mouth to taste followed by the toasted cheese sandwich

Wally Style . . . a poem

The Wally wears a duffle coat
The Wally wears a mac
The Wally wears a donkey jacket
With 'Council' on the back.

The Wally wears flared trousers
The Wally wears pink socks
The Wally wears green underpants
And hangs around the docks.

The Wally wears bri-nylon shirts
The Wally wears sou'westers
The Wally wears a beenie cap
And looks like Charlie Chester.

What the Well-dressed Wally Wears

* Rubber insoles
* Coloured clogs
* Pullovers with a sporting motif on the left breast pocket
* Underpants with a saucy message on the front
* Crimplene trousers
* Patterned socks
* Elastic garters
* White bri-nylon shirts
* Women's stretch trousers with the bit at the bottom to go around the foot
* Zip-up jumpers
* Shirts that carry the label 'Elegance' or 'Male Sophistication' and cost £2.45 from Redditch Saturday Market
* Monkey-nut trousers, with the pockets in the knees
* Bobble hat with loose bobble that bounces around the head when you move
* Dark blue gaberdine raincoat with a brown belt
* Short socks that slip down inside the shoe the moment you move in them
* Any item of surgical wear
* Ex-army style pullovers, with suede patches on the elbows and shoulders
* Rally anoraks made in Singapore
* Lumberjack jackets with lots of things in the pockets
* Second-hand plimsolls

Popular Music

Generally speaking, Wallies only enjoy music other people have long since forgotten about: The Bay City Rollers, The Osmonds and The Brotherhood of Man are all top recording Wally artists. Many Wallies never develop musically beyond the 'Easy Listening Section' and will only buy records marked '50% off recommended price plus second record free inside'. Most Wally records are bought at station bookstalls and airport terminals. Excellent examples of this type of record are: 'The Hollies sing Bob Dylan'; 'The Songs of The Rolling Stones By Other Artists' (look for the picture of a pouting lady on the front); and the 'Anthology of the Beverly Sisters' (a 36-record box set produced exclusively for the Readers Digest and not available through any other outlet).

By contrast, having spent virtually nothing on their records, most Wallies will spend extraordinary amounts when buying a system on which to play their music. Especially popular are systems with several hundred knobs, none of which produce a notable change to the sound.

Classic Wally artists to look out for now include:

* Shakin' Stevens
  Sheena Easton
  The Stranglers
  Bucks Fizz
  Queen
  Cliff Richard

Wally Home Furnishing

* Coffee table with screw-in legs that come off the moment anyone puts something fragile on top. Look for examples with antique-type map of the world on the top

* Flock wallpaper

* Table lamps made from empty bottles of Chianti

* Bedroom doors with little signs that say 'Gary's Room', and 'Dawn's room' and 'Trevor's Room', and have a picture of Snoopy alongside the name

* Combined sideboard and radio-grams

* Corner bar with deep-buttoned, simulated leather front and genuine optics behind

* Wicker wastepaper bin in the shape of a rabbit

* Curtains that don't quite meet in the centre

* Three-piece leatherette suites that fall over backwards when anyone sits on them

* Hearth rug with a pattern of a Spanish galleon

* Carriage lamps anywhere at all

* Elegant electric fires with an authentic coal-effect glow

* Coat hooks that come away from the wall as soon as you put anything on them, taking with them an old rawlplug and five square inches of plaster

* Wall cornices for mock alabaster busts of people no-one has ever heard of

The Wally's Favourite TV Programmes

THE TOP TEN!

1. *3-2-1*
2. *Family Fortunes*
3. *Game For A Laugh*
4. *Kick Start*
* 5. *Magnum*
6. *Closedown*
7. *Juliet Bravo*
* 8. *The Dukes of Hazzard*
9. *Pebble Mill At One*
10. *Name That Tune!*

BOUND VOLUMES T.V. TIMES

Wallies In Love

Wallies, as a rule, do not fall passionately in love, finding sexual arousal confined to a short period in late puberty (a three-to-four-week period between 25½ and 26).

When aroused, Wallies tend to show severe skin irritation and laugh volubly in a funny high-pitched squeak. After this initial response, Wallies confine themselves to occasional covetous blushes and a somewhat marked increase in the number of trips to the toilet.

Most Wallies tend not to fall in love because of three things, which is as good a reason as any for not falling in love. What's more, Wallies who do find themselves in love tend to become extremely hot and clammy beneath their quilted anoraks and nylon underwear, with the result that any embrace runs the risk of slippage and an ensuing accident.

Wallies who do fall in love are advised to see their doctor or, if he or she is too attractive, to see someone who works for the Central Electricity Generating Board who is almost certain to hold no sexual appeal whatsoever, even to a Wally, thereby destroying any lingering sexual urges.

Romantic Things for Wallies to Say

* Do you always walk with a limp?

* Would you like to come upstairs and see my collection of Matchbox Models of Yesteryear/John Travolta Souvenirs?

* Are you sitting on my banana sandwich?

* You've got lovely big teeth

* Was that your cat I just trod on?

* I think I'm going to be sick

* You don't sweat a lot for a fat man do you?

* I think I may have a contagious disease

* My mother used to have a coat like that during the war

* Would you like to have a lick of my lolly, if you lick this side there's a bit where I haven't sucked all the juice out yet

The Life Hereafter

When the reaper comes a reaping,
When the Lord of Darkness calls,
When at last they blow the candle,
I won't be there to greet them
Because I'll have probably just popped out
To a Little Chef for a bite to eat.

Adrian

The Wally Hereafter

Few people are certain of what happens to the Wally in the life hereafter. Re-incarnation is a popular belief, with ants, insects, small fish and traffic wardens the most popular suggestions.

Also common is the belief that they will be taken away to another planet in a giant silver-coloured space ship with flashing lights to become chief ruler of another galaxy. Those Wallies who do reconcile themselves to death can be remarkably phlegmatic about the whole affair. They may even promise to write or send a card as soon as they get there.

However it seems likely that few Wallies, if any, actually make it to either the upper or the lower chamber. Most will prefer to stand around 'inbetween', annoying passing souls of the dear-departed by loud and tuneless whistling, and by refusing to leave the Space Invader machines and let somebody else have a go.

The Wally Report

In 1981, the government completed its first-ever report on the Wally. The report, on nasty-thin-notepaper-that-tears-as-soon-as-you-touch-it and held together with a staple that completely missed two sheets and went clean through the other one, proved conclusively that Britain was dangerously overrun by Wallies, even more so than Finland or the Channel Islands. Among the many findings thrown up by the report were:

1. Over 84% of the sample population interviewed admitted to having watched *Blankety Blank* at some point in their lives.
2. Nearly 87% of people asked would recognise Tony Blackburn if they saw him in the street. A significant proportion would also run up and ask for his autograph.
3. Under 3% of the people questioned said they would go to see the doctor if they came into contact with a copy of the *Mail on Sunday*.
4. Over 50% of the cross-section polled said they would be happy to drive in an Austin Allegro even if it involved wearing a cap and smoking a pipe.
5. Nearly three-quarters of the people involved said they had heard of Rumbelows.

On the pages that follow we list case studies that were cited in that paper, which identify closely with classic examples of the Wally marque.

Simon Wet

Too insecure even to attend his own birth, Simon is believed to have been delivered by the midwife, in a darkened room, with the curtains tightly drawn, and with no-one else present.

Simon suffers from a chronic lack of confidence, and even finds it difficult to talk to himself without clamming up horribly with embarrassment. He was brought up in his late teens by a maiden aunt who taught him how to ride a tricycle with stabilisers attached and how to hold down an assistant manager's job with Barclays Bank for twenty-five years.

Simon lists his main interests as looking after his extensive collection of Football League programmes and eating strawberry-and-melon-flavoured yoghurt.

He is married and is trying to work out how you get children.

Miles O'Wally

Miles's hobbies are reading the *Daily Express*, calculating the compression ratios on his new Skoda Super Estelle and going round to the man next door to ask him if he can smell gas.

Since leaving the army in 1958, where he served as a quarter master in the soft-furnishing department, he has pursued a rich and varied career. For three years he had a very interesting job in the Spare Parts department of a firm of international Switch Gear manufacturers. He then joined a firm who manufactured the machines that manufactured the Switch Gear machinery, before finally deciding on a complete change and joining a firm that put the completed Switch Gear into little boxes with 'Switch Gear' written on the top in big letters with 'Parts Department' underneath in slightly smaller letters.

He drives an 'N' registration Morris Marina, with stick-on wire-effect hub caps, and his favourite clothing is an outsize, home-knit, Fair Isle sleeveless jumper with a bit of wool dangling down at the front. He lives in a dormer-bungalow near Redhill.

Donald Putrid

Lives in Leamington Spa with a cooker and two fridges. After leaving school Donald spent six months in the Accounts Office of a small road haulage company, but left when he found the hectic social life too hot to handle. Subsequently went into local government and stayed there for ten years, developing a keen interest in filing bits of paper, and cultivating a particularly dull and nasal voice.

He lists his likes as anything to do with Shirley Bassey, exotic cooking (especially Vesta meals) and aeromodelling post-war commercial airliners. His dislikes are sex and anything that involves taking his vest off.

Angus Barely-Functioning

Hails from north of the border. Inherited his mother's eyes, nose and beard, and his father's chin, forehead, lower abdomen, bicycle clips and Tayside castle.

Notable features of his life as a Wally include the complete coverage of all interior surfaces of the castle with mock teak-effect wallpaper and the subtle use of Olde-Worlde-style lamp shades depicting famous hunting scenes. Later editions to the house have included an 'Elizabethan style' solarium with matching jacuzzi in 'Jacobean effect' trim and the clever but discriminating use of genuine 'antique-type' up-and-over doors in the coachyard.

Angus drives a 1936 Bentley, with black vinyl roof and Go-faster stripes, and his favourite hobby is sitting in front of the 36″ colour television watching repeats of the *Perry Como Show*.

The Wally Year Planner

Most great planners are Wallies. Indeed, there is something exclusively Wally-like in drawing up elaborate plans on a large sheet of graph paper that then gets lost completely only to turn up two weeks after the last event on it should have taken place.

When planning your year ahead in this manner, try and use a wide variety of coloured crayons and pencils. Make sure some of these fail to write clearly. Also attempt to introduce elaborate codes and ciphers to the items on the planning chart to render the whole thing totally unworkable.

Hints on Your Year Planner

1. Always enter any event due to take place onto the chart as soon as it becomes a possibility. This will allow you to cross it out and re-enter it again any number of times over the next few weeks, thereby creating an ugly mass of scratchings and Snopake.
2. Always affix the chart to the wall in such a way that writing onto it clearly becomes an impossibility.
3. Always leave an empty felt tip pen handy beside the chart so that you have to lick the end several times to get it to write and so that you end up going over the whole thing four or five times in an effort to make it more legible.
4. Never do anything until you have referred to your planner.

On the following pages is a month-by-month list of Wally events you may care to add to your Year Planner when complete . . .

January

11th   World Convention of International Wallies, held in the foyer of the MFI Bargain Superstore, Luton.

18th   Wally Club Annual Awards. A series of yearly awards for advancement in the field of Wally behaviour, including: smiling at waste paper baskets; walking the wrong way through revolving doors; forgetting to remove socks whilst taking a shower; making pictures of racing cars at the dinner table using peas and gravy left over after everyone has been served; and licking all the stick off postage stamps so no-one can use them.

24th   Start of Neasden to Dollis Hill car race.

28th   Finish of Neasden to Dollis Hill car race.

31st   National 'Getting In The Way Of Other People At Bus Stops' Day.

February

2nd   Start of 'Revving Car Engines Up Loudly While Waiting at Zebra Crossings' Season.

4th   America founded by Wallies.

5th   America losted by Wallies.

8th   Demonstration by the Wally Club of the art of eating a runny boiled egg sandwich from out of a blue plastic lunch box without removing the greaseproof paper wrapping first.

20th   Darts International at the Glenn Hoddle Sports and Conference Centre, over the all-night launderette, Leyton High Road. And afterwards at the North London Teaching Hospital (Intensive Care Unit).

March

12th   Start of the most extensive-ever exhibition of unusual and exotic dangling dice. Mark II Ford Cortina drivers admitted free. Canvey Island, opposite the bus terminus. Ask for the man in the Starsky and Hutch cardigan with the buttons shaped like little footballs.

15th   Wallies Through the Ages. A pageant in words and dance as performed by the combined staffs of British Telecom South Eastern Region.

20th   Anniversary of the opening of the first ever branch of Milletts.

22nd   Attempt on the World Record for the longest ever consumption of a Rum n' Raisin Choc Ice (at present standing at 4 hours 22 minutes).

April

11th   Wallies from England, Scotland, Ireland and Wales compete in the annual 'Ilush Puppy Gents Slip On (With Laces That Are Just A Bit Too Short To Tie Properly)'. Prizes include a week for two in a National Coaches booking hall of your choice, a fur-lined toilet roll holder and a chance to win enough Fablon to last a lifetime.

19th   Wally Day of In-Action.

23rd   Wally Club Christmas Dinner.

25th   National 'Manage-To-Get-Your-Clothes-Soaking-Wet-Even-Though-It's-Perfectly-Dry-Outside' Day.

27th   Wally Club day trip to Australia.

May

1st   Start of the 'Putting Holiday Stickers For Places You've Never Been To In The Back Of The Car' Season.

8th   Anniversary of the invention of the green felt tip pen.

11th   'Wallies All Over The World'. Live link-up with Wally TV presenters in Belgium, Holland, New Zealand, Canada and Norway. Hosted by a man in a dark blue zip-up anorak with detachable hood and moonboots.

16th   Wallies everywhere remember those who gave their lives in the cause of The Wally by trying to consume the entire stock of individual fruit pies on British Rail buffet cars.

June

11th   Golden Jubilee of the introduction of Mock-Tudor style thermal cladding into Britain.

14th   The Wallies Outward Bound Club sets off for its annual mountaineering holiday in Lincolnshire.

21st   Ceremony in Bromsgrove town centre to commemorate the discovery of the hand-knitted hot-water bottle cover with a picture of Shakin' Stevens crocheted onto the front.

22nd   In a special tribute to Wallies, ITV start a major season of repeats of the *Benny Hill Show*.

30th   Anniversary ceremony to pay special tribute to the launching of the Yorkie bar.

July

3rd	On this day, 1956, the first ever man-powered flight was made by Dan Air.
7th	Sir Wally Raleigh brings back the prawn cocktail-flavoured potato crisp to England.
13th	Walking Over the Roofs of Parked Cars International: England versus Scotland.
14th	Walking Over the Roofs of Moving Cars on the Motorway International: Scotland versus Millwall.
21st	Wallies celebrate ten years of the Jackie Stewart racing driver cap.

August

14th   Party to honour birthday of the man who wrote the lyrics of the Birdie Song

15th   New form of contraceptive pill for Wallies due to be announced by the British Cardboard Box Company.

20th   Ipswich Cinema Club special gala evening – 'The Best of the Birds Eye Fish Finger Adverts'! A special chance for Wallies to see and enjoy again some of the best fish finger advertisements from the last twenty years.

26th   Start of the Vauxhall Viva Week with a special guest appearance from Matthew Kelly.

27th   The Ormskirk Ladies Slipper Baths Committee present a celebration in words and aromas of the Marks & Spencer quilted dressing gown. Also included in the performance is the son-et-lumière 'Pom-Pom Slippers Throughout The Ages'.

September

9th   International Year of the Roof Rack. Exhibitors from all over Huddersfield gather for this most prestigious of events.

12th   Anniversary of the opening of the Hanger Lane Gyratory System. Flat tyres and over-heated engines optional.

14th   Charity Car Horn Sounding Session followed by a motorcade through the streets of Hitchin to commemorate twelve and a half years of the Radio One Car Sun Strip.

18th   Street parties to celebrate the 86th Annual Confederation of the Society of People Called Graham.

21st   Pro-Am Sticking a Piece of Wire into a Faulty Plug Socket to See if It's Still Working, Chertsey Gardens.

24th   National Lego Construction Championships, seniors and veterans event. Also Subuteo and Scalextric events.

October

1st	The Grand Order of Wallies Formal Dinner Dance (Patron: Dave Lee Travis). Bring a bottle.
8th	*3-2-1* Omnibus Edition! Eighteen solid hours of the only programme on television dedicated solely to the Wally.
12th	Anniversary of the first ever Wally to become Chairman of British Steel.
14th	Juilo Iglesias Festival of Popular Music, New Street Station, Birmingham.
20th	Annual Wallies Versus the Rest, Indoor Power Boat Race (from the Municipal baths, Kettering).
24th	Wally Mastermind Final. Subjects include 'Cardigan and District Bus Timetables' and 'The History of the Toggle'.

November

1st   Wallies congregate on Coventry for the first convention of 'Other People Playing Songs of The Beatles on a Hammond Organ, While Wearing a Shirt Unbuttoned to the Waist with a Large Gold Medallion Dangling About Underneath'.

6th   Wallies up and down the country spend the day collecting burnt-out fireworks.

17th   Anniversary of the first ever showing of *Terry and June* on British Television.

20th   International 'Do You Think I Look A Bit Like That Bloke Out Of *Minder*' knock-out tournament.

24th   Attempt on the world speed record for unravelling a fully rolled toilet roll.

December

2nd   Last day for going out in a public place in the Bermuda shorts you've been wearing since August (not until the 27th in Scotland).

4th   Last day for buying 250 Christmas cards from Woolworths for 56p.

13th   Last day for using a complete roll of Sellotape to wrap up one small record token.

25th   Day on which all Wallies give each other Christmas presents they will never use and spend hours trying to remove the Turkey Stuffing they spilt inside the new electric salad tosser at dinner.

29th   Day on which all Wallies try to start their new Letts 'Wally Around Shopping Centres for Hours Trying to Find the Gents Toilets and Jumping Up and Down in Front of the Automatic Doors' diaries.

Wally Things to Do With This Page of the Book

1. Scribble all over it with a leaky blue biro, then tear it out and leave it where someone can sit on it.

2. Try to see how it is fastened to the other pages in the book by bending the whole thing along the spine and pulling it away from the cover.

A Special Page for Wallies Who Aren't Very Good at Reading

Revision Notes for the Previous Page

First published in Great Britain in 1984
by Century Publishing Co. Ltd,
Portland House,
12–13 Greek Street, London W1V 5LE

ISBN 0 7126 0473 1

Photoset by Deltatype, Ellesmere Port
Printed in Great Britain in 1984
by Richard Clay (The Chaucer Press) Ltd,
Bungay, Suffolk